IMAGES
of America

CORINTH

IMAGES
of America

CORINTH

Rachel A. Clothier

ARCADIA
PUBLISHING

Published by Arcadia Publishing
Charleston SC, Chicago IL, Portsmouth NH, San Francisco CA

Library of Congress Control Number: 2009926106

For all general information contact Arcadia Publishing at:
Telephone 843-853-2070
Fax 843-853-0044
E-mail sales@arcadiapublishing.com
For customer service and orders:
Toll-Free 1-888-313-2665

Visit us on the Internet at www.arcadiapublishing.com

*To all those who had the foresight
to save photographs and label them*

CONTENTS

ACKNOWLEDGMENTS

The town of Corinth is made up of a multitude of fascinating people, past and present, with countless stories to be told. Many people have helped collect and preserve these stories over the years. Genevieve Shorey Moore was an exceptional friend and fellow historian. Her encouragement and hard work helped to reactivate the Corinth Museum and preserve the town's amazing history. Her presence is greatly missed. Without the help of many people, this project would not have been possible. Ruth Allen, Mary Earls, Marcia Breakey, Edward Seaman, John and Edith Tooker, J. Douglas Anderson, Ernest Clothier, the photography skills of George Holland, and the late town historian Arthur Eggleston have all shared their time and knowledge with me. My family has given their enormous support to see this book to completion. My husband, Bryan, and daughter, Anne, are my greatest contributors. Thanks to the many others who offered encouragement and shared their interests with me.

It has been a challenge and a pleasure to research the photographs for this book. Some of these images have not been publicly viewed for generations, while others are on display at the Corinth Museum. Finding these photographic memories has been like a treasure hunt, a rich and enlightening discovery of Corinth's past. It should be noted that these images are a mere sampling of the many uncovered in the process of researching this publication. I challenge future generations to continue the historical research and help keep the stories alive.

Unless otherwise noted, the photographs appearing in this book are from the collection of the Corinth Museum.

INTRODUCTION

Corinth is located in the northern section of Saratoga County. The Hudson River forms the northeast border, and the southern Adirondack Mountains begin to rise in the western half of the town. The geography of the area makes it a likely spot for hunting and fishing. The river attracts wildlife and provides a ready transportation route. The mountains and valleys are rich in natural resources including virgin forests, cascading streams, and even a lost lead mine.

The features that brought the Native Americans here year after year are what attracted the first white settlers to this area, and the region was regularly traversed by the Iroquois Indians. One of their main trails north followed along the present-day Route 9N. The Dutch first laid claim to this part of the New World after Henry Hudson sailed up the Hudson River in 1609. Later the English gained control and began to divide their holdings into land grants or patents; the Kayaderosseras Patent was granted in 1708 and included much of this area. England wanted to capitalize on its property, and deeds were issued to encourage the settlement of the area and harvesting of natural resources for its benefit. Two brothers, Edward and Ebenezer Jessup, signed a document on behalf of themselves and other loyal subjects to take claim of over 40,000 acres of land along the upper Hudson River Valley in 1772. The Jessups were the first lumbermen in the area. Logs were cut in the north, chained together as rafts, and floated down the river to their sawmills. To avoid having the logs break up while going over the falls, they were landed and hauled by oxen to a place below the falls where they continued down the river. The site where the logs were taken out of the river became known as Jessup's Landing. Because the brothers were loyalists, they fled to Canada at the outbreak of the American Revolution. They took part in English raids on the Mohawk Valley. Edward Jessup eventually settled in Prescott, Ontario, and Ebenezer sailed to England and later to India, where he died in 1818.

Near the end of the American Revolution, the region became popular for settlement. Many families were anxious to move out of crowded New England and find farmland for new homesteads. Ambrose Clothier came to the area near Mount McGregor in the late 1770s and built his homestead. Joseph Eggleston also migrated to the area. He had intended to go to Luzerne, but his livestock scattered near the Clothier neighborhood, and he remained there for the rest of his days. Descendents of both of these families continue to live in the town.

The township now known as Corinth was originally parts of other towns. Prior to 1791, it was contained in the county of Albany in the district of Saratoga. Saratoga County was then separated from Albany. Corinth was a part of the town of Greenfield from 1793 until 1801. By 1801, Hadley was split from Greenfield. At this time, the Corinth community had a population of about 800. As the towns became more populated, the large tracts of land were divided into two or more townships, thus making governing easier. When it became evident that Hadley would be divided in 1818, members of the community gathered at Chapmanville, now South Corinth, to decide upon a name for their township. Mrs. Washington Chapman, whose husband kept a clothiery on the Kayaderosseras Creek, was given the honor of naming the town. She opened her Bible to the book of Corinthians and said, "There it is, it shall be called Corinth."

Corinth continued to grow, especially after the paper mill was established on the banks of the Hudson River at Palmer Falls. The Hudson River Pulp and Paper Company became a very profitable business, and in 1898, it joined with more than a dozen other paper mills to form the International Paper Company. Corinth became known chiefly as a mill town while small farms dotted the valley landscape. Other smaller businesses came and went, but it was believed the paper industry would last forever. This belief ended in 2002 when International Paper Company closed its Hudson River mill. As the mill site sits empty along the banks of the river, Corinth has become more of a bedroom community. Most of its residents are employed in other towns and commute to work. Many families come to the mountains and riverfront in the summer, swelling the population from Memorial Day until Labor Day.

One

THE EARLY YEARS

Between 1775 and 1800, the population of the area grew steadily. The Egglestons, Clothiers, Ides, Hodges, Grippens, Randalls, Cowles, Boardmans, Comstocks, Edwards, Parkmans, Eddys, Puquas, and many other families arrived. Several of the men were veterans of the American Revolution. They had seen part of the upper Hudson River while fighting the British at Saratoga and decided to return to settle. Tracts of land were claimed, and farmsteads were cleared. The earliest homes were rough log cabins. As families began to prosper, they built frame homes. Lumber mills were first built about 1800 along the Hudson River and at South Corinth. Daniel Boardman built a gristmill and store at Jessup's Landing before 1800. Communities were organized near the landing on the Hudson River and in the area around South Corinth. Both areas had a supply of fast-moving water to furnish power for mills. The town of Corinth was officially established in 1818. Farmers raised sheep for wool production, and woolen mills processed the raw material into fabric. The expansive forests of hemlock trees provided hemlock bark for use in the tannery business. The town remained very rural with small industries until the coming of the Adirondack Railroad in 1865. Within a few short years, a new industry came to town that changed the economy of the region.

Brothers Edward and Ebenezer Jessup operated a vast logging operation in the Adirondacks in the 1770s. The logs were tied together and floated down the Hudson River to a spot just above the falls where they were brought ashore and transported by oxen to below the falls and placed back in the river to continue to the sawmills downstream. This painting by Clara Mae Towers Orto is her interpretation of what Jessup's Landing may have looked like during those logging operations. Orto is a local artist who has painted several scenes of Corinth over the past 40 years.

Palmer Falls has a drop of over 90 feet. Cliffs rise up from the sides of the cataract as palisades. Waterpower was first harnessed here along the Hudson River in the early 1800s with the building of a sawmill. Later a gristmill and woolen mill also utilized the river. By 1830, Beriah Palmer purchased the property and water rights, thus giving the falls his name. The site remained idle until 1859 when Thomas Brown purchased the property.

Log cabins were the first permanent structures built by early settlers. Few windows were used because glass was expensive and hard to transport. Emmaline Clothier lived in this cabin, and when the photograph was taken around 1900, it had been standing for about a century. In the census records of 1855, a few log cabins were listed and their value was placed at $5. (Author's collection.)

11

Adam Comstock came to Corinth from Rhode Island after the American Revolution. He and his wife, Margaret McGregor, had 17 children and called this building home. It was constructed in 1788 and is considered the first frame house in Corinth. The building was converted to a corncrib after the larger house was erected.

This is the second frame house erected by Comstock. It was probably built about 1795 and was originally only one-and-a-half stories high. He died in 1819 and was buried in a small stone-walled cemetery on the property with many other members of his family. Later the property was sold to James Angell. He is purported to have enlarged the house to a full two stories.

The Joseph Eggleston house stands on Fuller Road and was built about 1790, replacing the original log structure that was erected there in 1775. Eggleston and members of his family are buried in a small cemetery opposite the end of Fuller Road on South Main Street. A larger Eggleston cemetery is less than a mile down the road, also on South Main Street.

One of the first families to settle in Corinth was the Clothiers. They built a log cabin near Mount McGregor. Ambrose Clothier and his wife, Mercy May, had four boys and four girls. One son, Asa, built a home below a hill near the Hudson River. This house was built about 1818 and stands at the end of Folts Road. (Courtesy of the Saratoga County Historian's Office.)

Levi Heath constructed this house about 1805. He married Lucy Lindsay in 1801, and they raised their 11 children here. One of their sons, Simon Heath, took over the farm and stayed here until 1870, when he moved to another farm down the road. The farm is currently owned by the Fenton family and is located on Fenton Road. (Courtesy of the Saratoga County Historian's Office.)

This boulder is located in the yard of the Heath home. The family story is it was used as a samp rock. Lucy Lindsay had used the depression in the rock to burn corncob ash to make baking soda in the early 1800s.

In the late 1700s, William Grippen came to the eastern part of Corinth from Columbia County. At the beginning of the 19th century, he built the red house that stands between Fuller and Gabriel Roads. In 1870, Simon and Ann Eliza Ide Heath moved here, and it has been owned by their descendents ever since. (Courtesy of Bryan Clothier.)

For many years during the late 1800s and early 1900s, the Heath family held an annual reunion at many homes in the area. The reunion seen here was held during the summer of 1913 at the home of Harrison and Maud Clothier. Harrison's mother was a Heath. Over 50 descendents of brothers Levi and Ira Heath attended.

The Randall and Mallery families were also early settlers to East Corinth. Dulcena Mallery Randall was a first-generation Corinthian. Her husband, Obed Randall, was also a child of an early settler. Dulcena and Obed were married in 1851. Four generations of the family are pictured here in 1913. From left to right are Dulcena Mallery Randall, Sarah J. Randall Guiles, Bessie Guiles Clothier, and Blanche May Clothier. (Courtesy of John and Edith Tooker.)

Eggleston Mills was located in the northwest section of the town. A sawmill, grocery store, tavern, dance hall, blacksmith shop, and a house were located here. The settlement was located on the Daley Creek near Davignon Road. Rufus Eggleston is seated third from right.

The Ezekial Angell homestead was located on Angel Road across from the Angell cemetery. The home was built in the early 1800s, and several generations of the Angell family lived here. In March 1938, a chimney fire destroyed the house.

Jonathan Hodges was a veteran of the American Revolution and moved here from Rhode Island. He first settled in the town of Greenfield, and after his wife's death in 1795, he moved farther north to Corinth. This house was built about 1810, and the property consisted of 200 acres. Other owners of this home include the Grippens, Folts, and Corapis. This house still stands at the corner of Folts Road and County Route 24.

The Elisha Wilson homestead stood on a now-abandoned road that led from the back of the old reservoir down to Route 9N. It is of basic vernacular construction with a center chimney. Wilson came to Corinth from Massachusetts with his wife, Eleanor, before 1820.

The oxcart was the common way of travel in the 1700s and 1800s. Oxen were more efficient than horses and more common. Chauncey Cowles is seen here riding down Main Street in the latter part of the 19th century.

A remnant of the stagecoach days still stands in South Corinth on Chapman Street. Frederick Parkman built an inn about 1796 along the old Native American trail that follows much of present-day Route 9N. This tavern became a popular stop along the plank toll road from Saratoga Springs to Corinth. A ballroom was part of the back section of the building. (Courtesy of Saratoga County Historian's Office.)

According to legend, this tree in front of the tavern was planted by Frederick Parkman in 1801. It measured 17 feet and four inches around. Four platforms were built in the tree, and artists painted scenic views from there. In 1933, the owner of the building cut the tree down for firewood and removed the section of the inn that contained the ballroom. (Courtesy of Mary Earls.)

This house stands on Gabriel Road and was built in the early 1800s. Over the years, it has been owned by the Ambler, Perry, Heath, Gabriel, and Hughes families. (Courtesy of the Saratoga County Historian's Office.)

This house is typical of early frame construction in Corinth. It was located on Miner Road in South Corinth and was the Miner family homestead. Ira Gray identified the people in this picture as Mrs. Horace Miner, Mrs. Ned Miner, Ned Miner, and Horace Miner. This photograph was taken in the latter half of the 19th century. (Courtesy of Mary Earls.)

Jeremiah Eddy was an early settler in South Corinth. He was the first blacksmith in the area and operated out of a portion of this building. Eventually the building was used as a store and run by Yates Barbour in the early 1900s. Pictured in front of the store from left to right are unidentified, Yates Barbour, Mrs. Barbour, Albert Barbour (with a horse), Mrs. Gardner Allen, Fred Ochs, George Ochs (sitting), and four unidentified people. Upstairs, only Emma Barbour is identified in the middle. (Courtesy of Mary Earls.)

Jonathan Duell brought his family to South Corinth in the 1790s. His descendents built this house in the early 1800s. The woman standing behind the fence is unidentified. Others pictured from left to right are Julia Densmore Duell, Mathilda Ainsworth Densmore, and Henry Densmore. (Courtesy of Mary Earls.)

The old mill house still stands in the middle of South Corinth. It dates from the very early 19th century. Behind it stood the old stables that housed the teamsters and their horses. The Sim Brown Sawmill and Novelty Works stood just north of the house and an old gristmill that dated to 1805. (Courtesy of the Saratoga County Historian's Office.)

This homestead is believed to have been built about 1810 and still stands on Miner Road. Harvey Eddy lived here his entire life. (Courtesy of the Saratoga County Historian's Office.)

One of the first businesses to be started at Jessup's Landing was the gristmill. Daniel Boardman built this mill about 1793, and it continued in operation into the middle of the 20th century. Sturdevan Creek provided waterpower by way of the short canal seen in the foreground of the picture. The farmers paid their bills to the miller with grain, at a cost of one bushel for every 10 ground. The mill had several owners, including Orlando Boardman, David and Beriah Rogers, Isaac Barber, and Zina Mallery. Eventually it was operated by William Burnham, Harry Burnham, and John Winslow and was known as the Burnham and Winslow Feed Mill. Winslow closed the feed store in 1966, and an arsonist burned down the building in 1967. This mill was located at the bend on Mill and Mallery Street. (Courtesy of Saratoga County Historian's Office.)

The Alexander D. Parmenter homestead, built in the early 1800s, was located on the corner of Maple and Main Streets. In the 1930s, it was jacked up and moved to West Maple Street, where it still stands. A laid-up stone well at the right of the house was used as a landmark for deed measurements in this part of the village. Parmenter operated a store next to the house, which was later sold to Seneca Ralph.

Darius Fenton built this house between 1810 and 1820. It passed into the Henry Raymond family before Theodore Elixman bought it in 1882. It was modernized about 1908. The house on the corner of Palmer Avenue and Main Street was later owned by the Dayton family and was demolished in 1964 to make way for a gasoline station.

Two

THE PAPER MILL

The largest stimulus for the expansion of the town of Corinth was the introduction of paper manufacturing at Palmer Falls. The Hudson River had been used for its waterpower and transportation of timber for nearly 100 years before this site was considered for a paper mill. In 1859, Thomas Brown came from Niagara Falls and purchased the area at Palmer Falls. He built a canal from the river to his mill to provide power for his edge tool factory and later a woolen mill. Then the site was purchased by the Hudson River Pulp and Paper Company. The use of wood pulp in the manufacture of paper was patented a few years earlier and was introduced at the Hudson River plant. Up until this time, a mixture of wood pulp and rags was the method used to produce paper. Albrecht Pagenstecher became the president of the company, and Warren Curtis was the superintendent. The paper mill continued to increase in size and output. Logs were still floated down the river to the mill, but other freight had to be hauled from the train station out Hamilton Avenue to the mill, a distance of over two miles. A branch railroad line was constructed in 1888 to the upper portion of the mill, and two years later, it was extended to the lower mill yard. The mill continued to prosper and expand. In 1898, the Hudson River Pulp and Paper Company was one of 20 mills from New England and New York that joined together to form the International Paper Company. The first labor strike started in 1910 and was quickly settled. Another strike in 1921 lasted five years. The Hudson River mill was considered the largest paper mill in the world by 1948, when a huge 50th year party was held. Another large paper machine, No. 11, was installed in 1958. The century celebration was held here in 1998. In June 2002, it was announced the last of the original mills that created International Paper was to be closed later in the year.

The incredible power of the Hudson River is seen here at Palmer Falls. A portion of the paper mill is visible at left. The river had the largest current in the spring after the snow melted and the rains came. At other times, during a drought, people could walk across the Hudson River on rocks and not get their feet wet.

Logs were sent down the rivers from the Adirondacks to the sawmills and paper mills. They would be imprinted with a marking hammer so that each one could be identified and sent to the mill it was intended for. This photograph was taken in front of the Ambrose C. Hickok farm that stood on River Road. The average number of logs removed per day was 1,550 in 1892.

This woolen mill was built in 1865 by Thomas Brown near Palmer Falls. Brown was accidently shot by his night watchman on the evening of November 7, 1869. He had stopped by to check on the mill, and after picking up an armful of cloth to take inside, he was seen by the watchman. Being hard of hearing, Brown never heard the call from the guard, so he did not stop. It was dusk, so the watchman could not see the identity of the man. One shot was fired, and Brown died soon after. One year later, the mill burned, was rebuilt, and then the property was purchased by the Hudson River Pulp and Paper Company.

International Paper Company's office still stands on Pine Street and was erected in the early 1900s. The building was also referred to as the time office. The sulphite tower and water tower can be seen to the left of the building.

Warren Curtis was born in Passaic, New Jersey, in 1837. His father had been involved in the paper making industry in Massachusetts, New Jersey, and New York. After extensive training in the manufacture of paper, he came to the Hudson River Mill at Palmer Falls to become treasurer and manager. He became very involved in local government, the school, and the Baptist Church. He died in 1913 and is buried in the Corinth Rural Cemetery.

Each spring, the logs that were cut during the winter in the Adirondack Mountains were floated downriver to the mill. One account from an 1892 Corinth newspaper tells how the 13-foot logs that were sent down from Indian River "covered the entire Hudson River for a mile, raised the river seven inches, and were packed in every conceivable position, as deep as the river, and as high as ten feet above the water."

Softwood pulp logs were continuously sent down the river until the early 1950s. The four-foot logs were ground into pulp for paper production.

The Hudson River Pulp and Paper Company began operations in 1869 along the banks of the river. This photograph from about 1890 shows the offices and some of the mill buildings. Ira Grey told that his brother Charles helped construct the large smoke stack, and as the workmen were finishing it, he stood on his head on top of it.

The Hudson River Pulp and Paper Company produced this lithograph in the mid-1890s. From this print, one can see the enormity of the paper mill. At this time, the mill had a daily production of 150 tons of newspaper, 100 tons of wood pulp, and 60 tons of sulphite pulp. (Courtesy of Saratoga County Historian's Office.)

The machine shop crew is shown outside of the Hudson River Pulp and Paper Company on November 23, 1897. Only two men in the group are identified. P. J. Fagan is seated in the first row on the left, and Mr. Quinn is in the second row second from the right.

The interior of the machine shop is pictured in 1897. It fabricated, repaired, and replaced parts of the mill's equipment. The line shafts that powered the metal lathes can be seen in the room.

Pictured is a line of rewinder machines that cut paper rolls to size. Tracks along the floor can be seen where wagons were pushed to move the heavy rolls.

One of the older paper machines is pictured with the crew beside it. Another machine was on the opposite wall. In the background is a wagon full of "broke," or the mistakes and ripped paper pieces from the machine. It was collected and fed back into the pulp to be reprocessed into more paper.

These workers at the International Paper Company in the early 1900s are posed in front of stacks of stone-ground wood pulp called laps. The Hudson River provided all the power for the wood grinders. These laps were stockpiled ahead for times when the river was low and less power was delivered. This process continued until the 1950s when electric grinders were installed and there was steady power available.

This image shows workmen standing in front of stockpiled mill laps. The small trolleylike wagon was used to move the laps to the grinding area. It took less power to grind these laps into pulp than it did for the wood grinding.

One of the paper machine rooms is shown at the mill. The pulp, a mixture of ground wood and sulphite, went into these machines and was formed into a continuous sheet of newsprint paper. As paper came off each machine, it was sampled for uniform strength and weight.

Another photograph of the paper machines shows the proper attire for hot summer days. Inside the machine room, the temperature reached well over 100 degrees. The sheets of newsprint paper dried uniformly by passing over steam-heated revolving drums. Many of the men worked barefoot at the mill.

On April 16, 1903, the American Federation of Labor (AFL) granted a certificate of affiliation to misters Marsellins, Alexander, Randall, Curry, Swift, Kelleher, Ducek, Durrigan, and Smith to create a trade and labor union at Palmer Falls. The document was signed by Samuel Gompers, president of the AFL. (Courtesy of Arthur Eggleston.)

The Palmer Local No. 7 International Brotherhood of Papermakers is shown at a rally. Maurice T. Jones was the president, Jeremiah T. Carey was the general president, and W. T. Sturdevan was the secretary of the union.

The strike at the Hudson River mill of International Paper Company commenced on March 7, 1910, when Cornelius O'Leary was discharged from the mill without explanation three days earlier. The International Paper Company refused to recognize the union and yield to its demands. The New York State Militia came to Corinth to help escort the strikebreakers into the mill.

The militia was brought to Corinth by train. The old train station is shown in the background. It was mutually agreed that the strike be terminated on May 21, 1910. After 10 weeks, the strikers agreed to return to work. Arbitrators had worked to come to a compromise, but the labor union was not pleased with the settlement. Another strike began in 1921 and lasted five years. No photographs have ever been found of that strike.

The worst flood in 50 years hit in March 1913. The lower end of Main Street flooded, and 150 feet of the International Paper Company dam was washed out at noon on March 26. The mill was closed for several weeks until the dam could be replaced. This image shows the reconstruction of the dam near Palmer Falls in the spring of 1913.

Blacksmiths are shown at work making huge staples to be used in the rebuilding of the Palmer Falls dam. In the years following this flood, the New York State Legislature began working on a measure to prevent future disasters along the Hudson River. The Sacandaga Valley was deemed the best location to build a dam. The dedication of the Conklingville Dam and Sacandaga Reservoir was held on September 11, 1930.

The Adirondack Railroad began service to Corinth in 1865. The train stop was located west of the village on Hamilton Avenue. Industrial development increased after this time, although all freight to the paper mill had to be hauled more than two miles through the village. In 1888, a spur to the mill was opened. Freight was then taken directly to the paper company. After the coming of the trains, there was an increase in accidents and fatalities at the railroad crossings, and brush fires were an added concern due to the sparks coming from the locomotives. Water towers were erected to refill the steam engines. This picture shows a Delaware and Hudson Railway steam engine parked at the siding in Corinth. Eventually diesel locomotives replaced the steam-driven engines. When the mill closed in 2002, the train stopped coming into town. (Author's collection.)

Train accidents were all too common at the paper mill. Sometimes cars jumped the tracks, and other times brakes failed on the engine, causing the cars to go through a wall at the mill. This photograph shows an apparent collision, where some of the cars were crushed and the rolls of paper fell out.

This is an aerial view of the International Paper Company in the 1960s. Some of the piles of pulpwood can be seen at left. Concrete towers had spray nozzles mounted on them to wet the wood, preventing spontaneous combustion. The large building at left center is the commissary or Employee's Mutual Benefit Association (EMBA) building. It was constructed during the strike in the 1920s to house the strikebreakers. Palmer Avenue is in the front of the photograph, and Pine Street bisects the middle. The mill yard is shown in the rear.

Three

The Growth
of Corinth

During the early part of the 19th century, Corinth grew at a modest rate. Businesses were established, churches were founded, common schools were organized, and the local government met once a year to handle business. The population of Corinth increased with the success of the paper mill, and the 1890s saw a housing boom. Other industries related to the paper mill began to thrive. Services for the community were founded, including two fire companies, and the village of Corinth was established in 1886. Electricity was generated in the village beginning in 1896 but not after midnight or on moonlit evenings. The Corinth National Bank was formed in 1902. Four years later, the Corinth Telephone Exchange was in operation. It is no wonder that in 1913 Corinth was considered "one of the most up-to-date, most progressive and prosperous villages in northern New York." G. H. Wyman, the proprietor of the *Corinthian* newspaper also said, "Remember, if you fail to visit Corinth you will forever regret your mistake."

The Jessup's Landing map of 1856 shows the homes, businesses, and churches located in what is now called the village of Corinth. The north-south road is Main Street. The street in the center leading to the left is Maple Street, and the small portion of a street at the bottom right is Palmer Avenue. "S. H." denotes the schoolhouse. "B. S." is the abbreviation for blacksmith shop, and "W. S." denotes the wagon shop.

This is an overview of Palmer Avenue about 1900. The Presbyterian church can be seen at the left, and farther down the street, the steeple of the Immaculate Conception Church is seen rising above the tree line. The Melville house is in the lower-right side of the photograph.

42

The hotel at the corner of Main and Mallery Streets was the focal point of news during the Civil War. It was also the location of the post office during this time. The newspaper was read from the steps to keep the residents informed of the recent happenings. The hotel became known as Brady's and was destroyed in a fire on December 15, 1959.

The Central House stood for over a century and was considered a landmark of Corinth at the corner of Maple and Center Streets. It was advertised as giving special attention to commercial men. In 1913, it bragged about having steam heat, baths, electric lights, and 26 rooms to rent. Rates were $2 to $2.50 per day. This hotel was destroyed by fire in October 1971.

The Palmer Falls Hotel was situated on the corner of Palmer Avenue and Sixth Street. The hotel had 30 rooms, and in 1906, the rates were $1 per day. In the early 1900s, the building was cut in half and part of it was moved down near the mill for a rooming house.

The Commercial Hotel, operated by H. R. Kathan, was a very respectable establishment in the late 1890s. It stood on the corner of Maple Street and Hamilton Avenue. This image shows three of the teachers who roomed there. The hotel's livery stable can be seen on the left side. Eventually the hotel was made into apartments, and after a fire in 1983, it was demolished.

Ezra Sayre operated a drugstore here on Maple Street beginning in the early 1900s. Pictured on the upstairs porch are Dr. F. A. Smith and his two daughters. Standing below are Frank Woodcock (with a shovel), W. J. Pitkin, Edgar Costello, Lela Andrew, Bertha Costello, Clark Lillibridge, Sayre, and Dr. Charles B. Mallery. This drugstore was later operated by Gilmore and Zeh, by Howard Russell, and then by Carl Lawrence. The building is now home to a Chinese restaurant.

The Pitkin brothers came to Corinth from Schroon Lake in the late 1890s and opened a store on the corner of Maple and Center Streets. The post office was located at the rear of the building. This image shows the building decorated for a patriotic celebration. By 1901, John H. and Walter J. Pitkin were so successful that they erected a large, three-story brick store right in the center of the village.

Located in the center of town, the Pitkin building shows how prosperous the community had become by 1901. The main floor of the Pitkin building contained the store and Corinth National Bank. Farther up on the Main Street side of the building, smaller shops, including a jewelry store and a barber, rented space. The second floor had offices, and apartments were on the third floor. The building was razed in the early 1970s to make way for a bank and large parking lot.

The Pitkin store was the largest building in Corinth and was constructed by E. K. Thomas. It advertised being five stores in one, selling dry goods, clothing, shoes, crockery, and groceries. Posing for this interior photograph are, from left to right, John H. Pitkin, Elmer Bogle Jr., and Elmer Bogle Sr.

46

The Mallery block stood across Main Street from the Pitkin store. This three-story brick building contained the studio of photographer James Betts and two separate attorneys' offices on the upper floors. On the main level, a dry goods store called the Racket was on the left and K. Needelman, a merchant tailor, was on the right. This building burned in 1899.

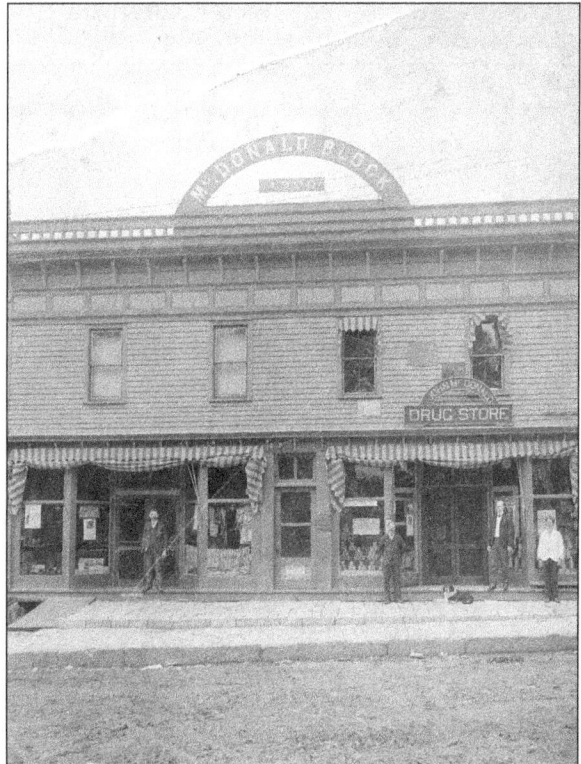

The McDonald block was constructed on the site of the Mallery building in 1901. John McDonald, owner of the building, operated his drugstore on the right side, and W. H. McRory's clothing store was to the left. This building burned on November 5, 1921, due to a defective electric light wire in the clothing store. The total loss of the building was estimated to be $5,000.

47

This interior image of the McDonald drugstore shows John McDonald at the right. He had a shop at his house where he blended many of the medicines that he sold. The store also contained a soda fountain, seen at left.

This view is looking down Maple Street toward the center of town. The Shorey building is being erected on the site of the recently destroyed McDonald block. The new structure was later known as the Proller building and then later referred to as the Densmore building. In February 2008, the entire block burned down.

The Herridon and Grippen store was located on the corner of Sherman Avenue and Main Street. This clothing store carried suits, overcoats, shirts, stockings, hats, caps, gloves, boots, and shoes. The building has also been known as the Belvidere Bar and most recently as Molly's Mason Jar Restaurant.

The early morning hours of February 11, 2008, saw the destruction of the main business block of Corinth. The fire started in the Densmore building and spread north to Sherman Avenue, taking three businesses with it. The Densmore Furniture store, a tattoo parlor, and Molly's Mason Jar Restaurant were destroyed.

Henry R. Woodcock's Harness Shop was a long-running business on Main Street. He was a dealer in harness, horse goods, robes, blankets, and whips. Handmade harnesses were his specialty. He also did boot and shoe repair. Shown in the photograph are Woodcock and his son.

Isaac R. Densmore conducted an undertaking business and furniture store on Main Street. He had the building constructed in 1893. His father Ransford Densmore started the business in South Corinth after the Civil War. Isaac moved to the village of Corinth to expand the business. The Densmore Funeral Home has been in the family for five generations. This building was demolished in 1982 to make way for the Corinth Commons apartment complex.

Arthur Young's meat market stood on the site of the Saratoga National Bank on Main Street. The meat market preceded the Pitkin building erected in 1901. Clifton Whitmore is driving the wagon belonging to R. M. Billings. (Courtesy of Thelma Scott.)

Leroy "Buck" Mallery (left) and William Mosher are shown behind the meat case at Mallery's Meat Market about 1930. The shop was located on Main Street on the site of the current village hall.

The Elixman Core Company was begun by Theodore Elixman in 1913. He held the patent for paper cores, which had special clips to fit the paper machines, and he had been manager of the Hudson River Pulp and Paper Company. The Elixman business closed in 1976, and the building was torn down in 1982 to make way for the Cumberland Farms Market on the corner of Maple and Center Streets.

Corinth Motor Company was located at the curve where Saratoga Avenue becomes Maple Street. Pictured from left to right are Frank St. John, Hamilton St. John, Stubby Denton, and Lyle Howland. The enterprise serviced cars and sold Socony gasoline. The building currently is Cleveland Brothers Landscaping.

The Corinth Shirt Factory was located on Mill Street and was started by John H. and Walter J. Pitkin in the 1890s. The company first used steam engines to supply power to the sewing machines. Cluett Peabody Company of Troy bought the business in 1899, and the factory closed in 1975.

A Christmas party was held at Cluett Peabody Shirt Factory in Corinth about 1930. By the 1940s, about 250 women worked at the mill. Women were paid 21¢ per dozen pockets sewn on shirts. Most of the women lived in the neighborhood of the mill and went home for lunch. After-hours parties were popular, and for special occasions, a turkey dinner was held in the cafeteria downstairs.

The Grand Union store was located on Main Street next to the Economy store in the 1930s. At that time, fancy fresh fowl cost 25¢ a pound; pork loins were 23¢ a pound; and tomatoes, beans, and peas sold at 10 cans for 59¢. This building is currently home of Rocco's Pizza.

J. Judd Dayton operated a jewelry store on Main Street on the lower level of the Pitkin building. This image shows his extensive inventory of watches and silverware. Dayton is pictured behind the counter ready for business.

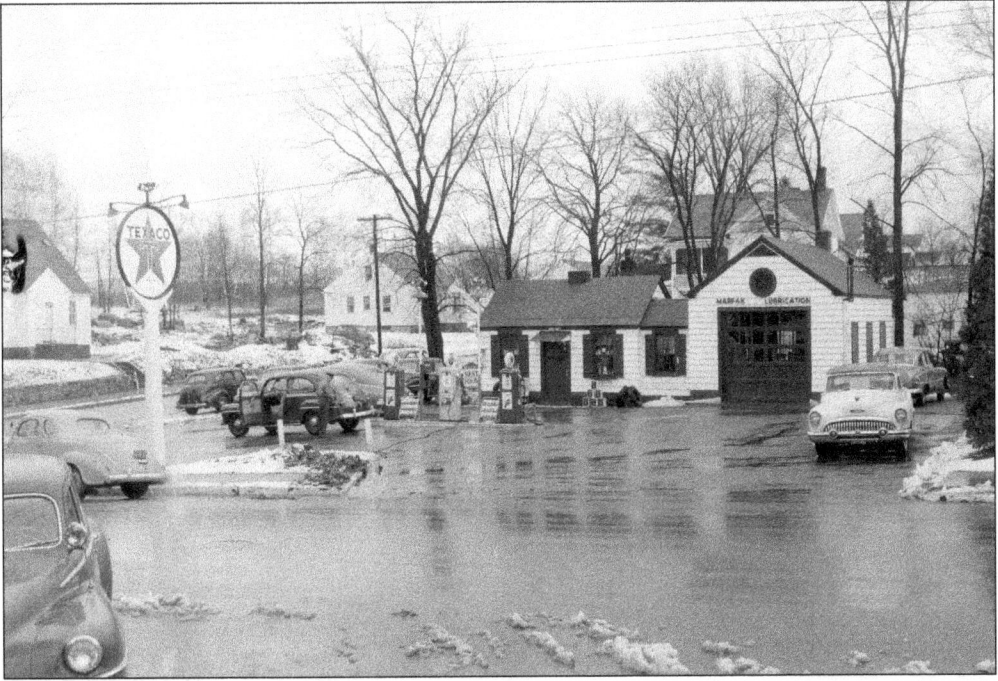

George Mott's Texaco Filling Station was located on the corner of Palmer Avenue and Heath Street. He was noted for keeping his service station neat as a pin, with flowers decorating the corner in the summer. This image was taken in March 1954.

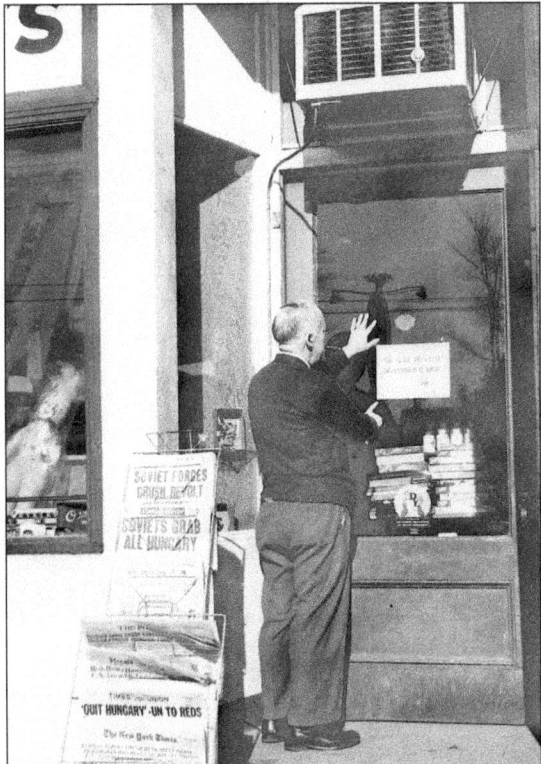

Edward Connolly is seen hanging a notice to "Be sure to vote! November 6, 1956," on the door of his pharmacy on Palmer Avenue. The newspaper headlines feature stories about the Hungarian Revolt. Connolly was the proprietor of this drugstore from 1923 until 1959. Donald McCarty operated the business after him.

The Sturdevan Weaving Factory and later bottling house stood on Mill Street in the late 1800s. When this photograph was taken, it was a carpenter shop. The upper portions of the building do not appear in very good repair at this point.

The E. H. Benway and Company Excelsior and Woodenware Mill was constructed in 1903 near the railroad tracks and depot on Hamilton Avenue. The mill was run by a 75-horsepower steam engine and was fully electrified. Excelsior was a type of wood shaving used as a cushioning packaging material. The mill burned a short time after opening, was rebuilt, but ceased operations by 1915.

The First Baptist Church of Corinth was organized on August 20, 1795, by seven men. Daniel Boardman was the elder and its first pastor. The wooden church was destroyed by a fire in 1897, and this brick edifice was dedicated on March 23, 1898. In the 1930s, the parsonage was built next to the church where the horse shed had been. The parsonage building was a house kit purchased precut and delivered to the site by train. The Baptist congregation sold the building and moved to a new church on Antone Mountain Road. (Courtesy of John and Edith Tooker.)

Members of the First Baptist Church Sunday school gather outside the parish for their picture in the 1960s. The church had two buses to pick up families for services. The Dayton house can be seen in the background. It is currently the site of a Rite Aid drugstore.

The Presbyterian Church was formed in 1814. Nezer Scofield and Edmund Sherman were the first deacons. The first church building was constructed on land next to the Sturdevan Creek purchased from David and Beriah Rogers for $70 in 1832. By 1852, the membership had dwindled, and the congregation ceased to function. Matthew Owens bought the property for $300 and converted the church to a private residence. This image shows the building shortly after it was made into a home.

By 1872, a new church was completed on Palmer Avenue on land donated by the Palmer Estate. The Presbyterian church had to be moved several feet in 1888 when the railroad spur to the paper mill was constructed. A pipe organ was donated by Theodore Elixman in 1895, and this necessitated an addition to be built on the back. The brick manse next door was erected in 1899 and is now used for the church activities.

The First Methodist Church of Corinth traces its roots back to the late 1820s when six members met to organize it. For the next three decades, they met in the school or in the Presbyterian church building. In 1858, the church was built on Main Street, and several improvements and expansions were done on the building.

Members of the First Methodist Church pose for the photographer outside the parish. The pastor at this time was Leonard Bard, who served in the pulpit from 1935 until 1940. A few years before this picture was taken, the church had new windows installed, along with an altar, a new pipe organ, a choir loft, and a dining hall.

The Church of the Immaculate Conception is located on Palmer Avenue. The parish hall was the original church erected in 1886. When the congregation outgrew the wooden structure, it was moved 70 feet to the west and a larger brick church was built.

In 1904, the Church of the Immaculate Conception congregation decided to construct a larger building. This image shows the laying of the cornerstone on Sunday, August 6, 1905, with the Very Reverend John Joseph Swift, vicar general of the diocese of Albany, officiating. More than 1,500 people attended the ceremony.

The Wesleyan Methodist Church of East Corinth stood near the foot of Wilton Mountain near the end of South Main Street. The church was built in 1892, and the formal dedication took place on January 25, 1893. It resembled a one-room schoolhouse, with a high ceiling and an alcove for the pulpit. The building sat vacant during the 1930s, and it collapsed in the 1940s.

The Wesleyan Methodist Church of Corinth was organized in 1900, and the congregation met in Prohibition Hall until 1902, when a parish was erected on property donated by Theodore Elixman. A second church building was completed, and the dedication was held on April 7, 1968.

Beginning in 1867, long before they had a church building, the Free Methodists met over a store on Main Street. Rev. Daniel St. Clair organized the services. The Free Methodist Church was dedicated in 1894 on Hamilton Avenue. In 1948, the church was moved across the street to its current site.

The South Corinth Methodist Church was erected in 1854 and is the oldest church building in the town of Corinth. The farmers in the congregation built the structure. An addition to the church was constructed in 1917.

The Rock School, district No. 4, was the first frame schoolhouse in Corinth and was built in 1811 on Eastern Avenue near a rock outcropping, thus the name. When the road was straightened in the early 1900s, the school was moved to the corner of County Route 24 and Fuller Road, where it still stands. This image is from about 1930.

The Kendall School, district No. 6, is located at the base of West Mountain on County Route 10. In 1908, the teacher was Stephen John Eggleston, and he is pictured at the far right in the back row. Other family names in the picture include Barrass, Hopkins, Wheaton, Andrews, Clothier, Reed, and Young. The building is now a private residence.

The Randall School District was also once called the Munroe District. This schoolhouse once stood at the intersection of South Main Street and Hollister Road. It was known as district No. 3 and was built sometime prior to 1855. The building was later converted to a private residence and suffered a fire. In the winter of 1993–1994, snow collapsed the roof. (Courtesy of John and Edith Tooker.)

A rare interior view of the Randall School is pictured. One teacher instructed first through eighth grades. (Courtesy of John and Edith Tooker.)

The first schoolhouse in Palmer was located on Palmer Avenue near the present brick school building. It is thought to have been moved to the mill yard and used as a storage facility. These 43 students posed on the front steps sometime prior to 1900.

The schoolhouse on Main Street was built in the mid-1800s. In this photograph, Electra Call is the teacher in the front row at left. By 1908, the Main Street School and the Palmer Avenue School had been constructed, and this building became the village hall for Corinth. The village offices have recently moved to a larger site.

This one-room schoolhouse, known as the Chapman School, was located in the center of South Corinth. (Courtesy of Mary Earls.)

The old district No. 1 school in South Corinth was built in the late 19th century, replacing the original one-room school. This building burned on February 5, 1934, and another school was erected on the site. (Courtesy of Mary Earls.)

The students of South Corinth district No. 1 pose for the photographer in the late 1890s. Some of familiar names on the school register at that time were Cote, Guiles, Earls, Ochs, Kendall, Eggleston, Wandell, Angell, and Atwell.

The district No. 8 school was located at Jenny Lake on West Mountain Road. Some of the teachers at this school were Willard Andrews, Susie Gray, Ethel Parker, Eunice Vail, and Roy Edwards. The building was later moved across the Hudson River and became a private residence.

Corinth High School was erected in 1891 and stood until 1958. It was a modern building for its time. At a cost of $20,000, the school contained eight classrooms, an auditorium, a library, a principal's office, cloak rooms, and a basement. In 1893, Dr. A. M. Hollister was appointed

principal at a salary of $1,000 a year. The building was demolished in 1958 to make way for the addition of a gymnasium to the new school.

The first class to graduate from the new high school did so in 1895. Standing from left to right are Clara Wagner, Hattie Carlton, Ida Early, and Clara Frank. Robert Branch is seated at center.

Members of the Corinth High School faculty sat for their picture about 1904. The teachers from left to right are (first row) Annie Scrafford, Lena Martindell, Lillian Gross, and two unidentified; (second row) Stella Wood, Mary Hickok, Dr. A. M. Hollister, Elinor Rogan, and Annis Perry; (third row) Mabel Sayre, Ella O'Brien, Mrs. Emer Perkins, Ida Burrett, and unidentified.

The members of the Corinth School Board were photographed about 1900. From left to right are (first row) Joseph Ross, Ambrose Hickok, Mr. Carey, and Theodore Elixman; (second row) William Burnham, Ezra Sayre, and E. K. Thomas.

Field trips were as popular with students a century ago as they are today. On May 1, 1903, the feldspar mines on West Mountain were the destination of a geology class directed by Dr. A. M. Hollister, the principal. The students attending include Grace ?, Mabel Pitkin, Ella O'Brien, Meta Gast, Anna Sims, Grace Hunt, Verna Tripp, Helen Craig, Lucy Craig, Anna Chase, Harry S. Shorey, Marcus Cronin, William Bates, Harold Bates, Harry Densmore, Victor Parmenter, and Howard Pitkin.

The students of grade 8a posed on the steps of Corinth High School in 1927 or 1928. From left to right are (first row) Jane Andrew, Kay Woodcock, Virginia Benton, Mildred DeLong, Jack Moylan, Bill Mayhew, Wyllis Dunham, Francis Cancro, and Percy Wendel; (second row) teacher Irene St. John, Marguerite Cahill, Agnes White, Betty Ingraham, Nicky Arganziano, Bud Ahearn, Harley Clothier, Dan Donlon, and DeVere Varney.

New Union Free School No.2, Corinth, N.Y.

The Union Free School No. 2 is now known as the Main Street School. It was built in 1908 on the site of the old burial ground that was moved to the Corinth Rural Cemetery in 1897.

UNION FREE SCHOOL, No.3, CORINTH, N.Y.

The Union Free School No. 3 is the building now known as the Palmer Avenue School. It has the same architecture as the Main Street School. The two structures were built for a cost of $30,000 in 1908. The Union Free School is now divided into apartments.

Pictured here in 1956, Corinth was outgrowing the existing high school facilities on Oak Street. In the background is the old high school, which was torn down in 1958. The addition to the right was built in 1936. Shown in the groundbreaking ceremony from left to right are Van Bloodgood, Mildred Fuller Mosher, Walter Green, Lewis Bartlett, Frank McCourt (with the shovel), Max Parmenter, Edward Connolly, and William D. Banks.

This aerial view of the Corinth High School on Oak Street was taken as the finishing work was being done on the expanded buildings in 1958. The name Corinth was painted on the roof as a landmark for pilots.

In February 1957, Corinth High School seniors visited the International Paper Company in connection with the EMBA annual essay contest. The class members looking over the mill, from left to right, are Curtis Williams, Gary Rowland, John Cernak, John Prestera, Kenneth Parker, Thomas Normile, Edward Whitaker, and Donald Eddy.

The 1957 Corinth High School graduating class listens to the Corinth High School Band under the direction of Richard Smaldone. Behind the graduates stands the American Legion Hall, which was later removed in order to enlarge the athletic field.

Mayor Victor A. Parmenter is shown throwing out the first pitch of the season at an early-1950s baseball game. The Main Street School is at left.

Corinth High School sports teams have received many honors over the years. In 1930, the basketball team took top honors. The players from left to right are (first row) Nicky Argenziano, Jack Arehart, Keith Spotswood, Sam Proller, and Phil Newton; (second row) Earl ?, Bud Ahearn, Duell MacIntyre, Paul Kehoe, Chuck Ingraham, Louis Sutliff, and Mr. Beckman.

A scene along Sherman Avenue looking west in the village is pictured. In the 1860s, a house was located at the end of the road near the corner of River Street. The first iron bridge was at the end of Sherman Avenue.

Electric Light Power House, Corinth, N. Y.

The Electric Light Powerhouse was also known as the Curtis Mill. It is located on the Hudson River near River Street. The International Paper Company took over the mill about 1928, and it was the power source for the company.

A convalescent home and hospital were first opened in Corinth in a brick home on Main Street in 1935 by Cecil Mae Winslow and Margaret Lovas, with help from Mrs. Harry Peterson. The health facility remained here for three years. The building is now a private residence. (Courtesy of Howard Russell.)

In 1938, the home of the late Warren Curtis and his wife, Margaret Parmenter Curtis, was given to the community by their daughters Mrs. Yates and Mrs. Bensel for use as a hospital. The home was located on Palmer Avenue. A new wing was added in 1960, which later became the Corinth Town Hall. The original house portion of the hospital was demolished in 1972.

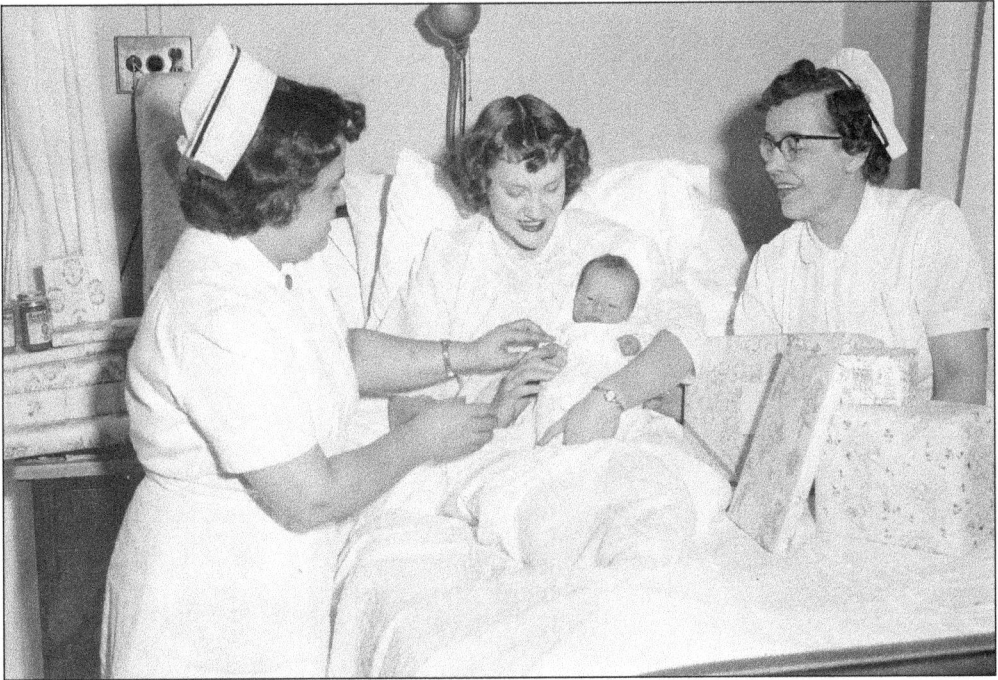

This is the first baby born at Corinth's hospital in 1957. Pictured from left to right are nurse Josephine Frasier, Mrs. Howard Dudley Holland, Raymond Holland, and hospital superintendent Mrs. F. T. Schermerhorn.

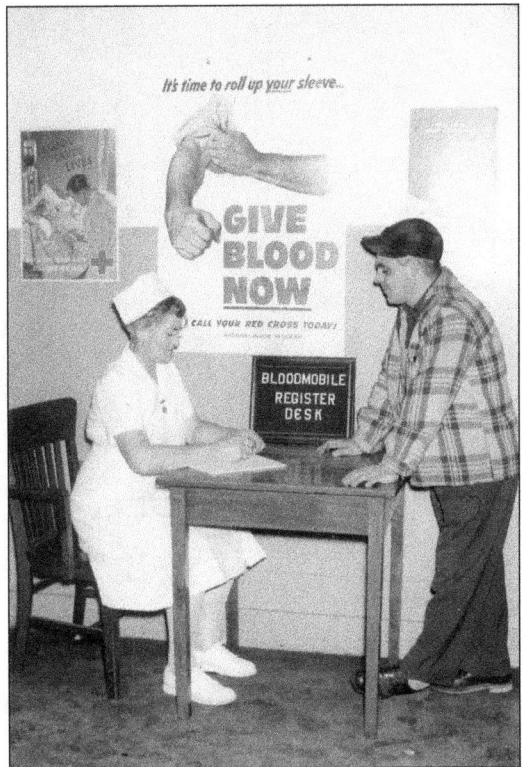

Mrs. Richard Rowley registers Anthony Manitta for a blood donation while at the International Paper Company, where he is employed. The blood drive was held at the Corinth High School on November 10, 1954.

The Corinth Emergency Squad was organized on March 8, 1946, and was incorporated three years later. Don Frazier and Frank Pountain pose in front of the ambulance at its parking spot at International Paper Company in 1947.

The Elixman Hose Company was formed in June 1895 and named in honor of Theodore Elixman, the secretary of the Hudson River Pulp and Paper Company. The hose company organized a drill team in 1898 and won several awards throughout the state. It was consolidated with the Warren Curtis Hose Company in 1934 to become the Corinth Fire Company.

The Elixman Hose Company No. 1 is lined up for a parade in front of Mallery's Meat Market on Main Street in the early 1900s. The brick Mallery house is seen in the right rear of the photograph.

Members of the Elixman Hose Company pose in front of a building on Main Street about 1900. John P. Brown, the foreman of the fire company, is standing in the back row on the left. In 1900, a fire broke out in the building where they held their meetings, and they lost all their records, awards, and other items.

The hose tower for the Elixman Hose Company stood behind the village school on Main Street. The school later became the village hall. After each use, the hose had to be hung up to dry. In this image, the men are erecting the tower using scaffolding.

The Warren Curtis Hose Company No. 2 was organized on June 22, 1895, at the Union House on Palmer Avenue. The company was named in honor of Warren Curtis, the manager and treasurer of the Hudson River Pulp and Paper Company. Because of its proximity to the paper mill, the firefighters have fought many blazes there and saved many lives. The hose company voted to attend the San Francisco Panama Exposition in 1915.

The Corinth Telephone Exchange was located on the corner of Main and River Streets. George Mason Jr. created the first telephone service in Corinth in 1891 when he wired a line between a shed and a barn at his home on Hamilton Avenue. Within 20 years, the exchange had grown to provide service to most of the businesses and private homes in town. Pictured in front of the building are Mr. Drake next to his shoe shop and Mason next to the telephone office. An early telephone operator is pictured at the switchboard. In 1953, the business was sold to General Telephone Company of upstate New York.

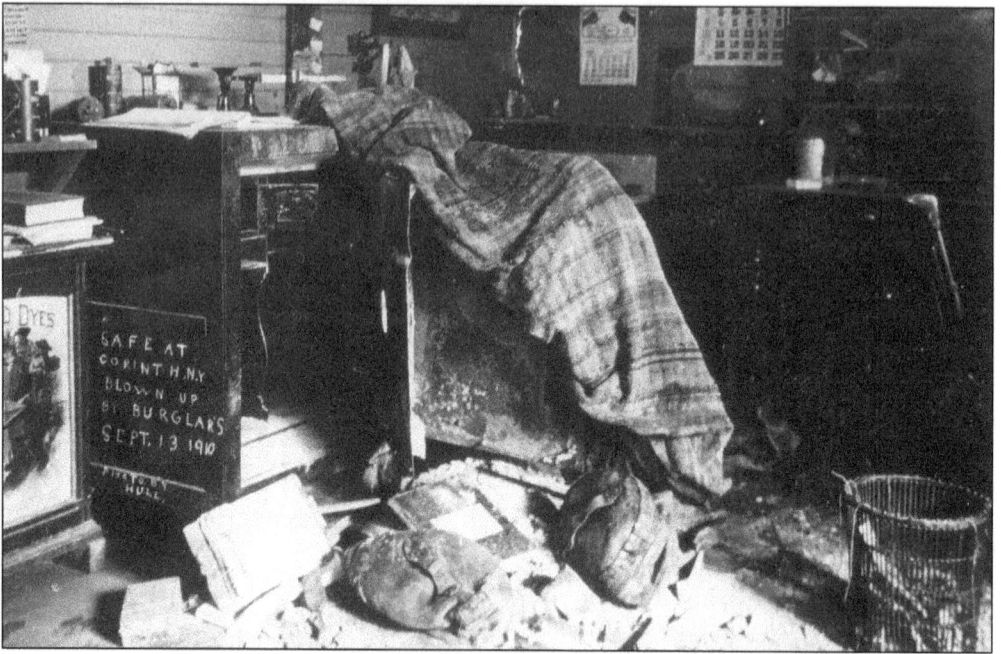

Postmaster Ezra Sayre was shocked when he opened his post office on September 14, 1910, to find robbers had broken in the night before. Nitroglycerine was used to blow open the safe, and $400 in cash and $300 in stamps had been stolen. No one was ever arrested for the crime. The post office was located on Center Street at this time.

This open truck was a familiar sight around Corinth in 1918. The truck was used by International Paper Company to haul wood and freight. (Courtesy of J. Douglas Anderson.)

Clearing Main Street of snow in the late 1920s was hard work. The Linn truck had two men operating the angle of the blades on the back. They are Jimmy Kenyon (left) and R. Brogue. Elmer Bogle stands behind the front blade.

The first bridge across the Hudson River at Corinth was opened in 1896. Clark Randall and William Snyder were the chief builders of this iron girder bridge. It was in use until 1952, when a new span was constructed. The Curtis Mill can be seen beyond the bridge, and the high school is visible on the hill.

The first sewer pipes were laid in the village in 1901. The sewage disposal septic tank was completed that year, and J. S. Mott and Sons were the civil engineers. The reservoir had been completed a few years before this. Up until this time, polluted water had been a problem in Corinth. A diphtheria epidemic hit town in 1892, and contaminated water from many wells and troughs was to blame.

The Spruce Mountain Fire Tower still stands in South Corinth. Erected in 1928, it was used for locating and observing forest fires in northern Saratoga County and the surrounding area until it closed in 1988. A hiking trail is now open to the tower. This photograph was taken by Bryan Clothier, the last observer at the tower from 1979 until 1988.

Levi Dedrick and family are pictured outside the home he purchased in 1885. This was the original Presbyterian church in Corinth, which was constructed in the 1830s, sold to Matthew Owens in 1867, and converted to a private residence by him. Dedrick operated a small shop in front of the house, where he sold carpets made by his wife, window shades, wallpaper, and hassocks. He did interior and exterior designing of residences as well as picture framing. The family also rented out rooms in the house to boarders. Dedrick's daughter Anna Dedrick Lincoln lived nearly a century in this home. It was demolished in 1993 to provide additional parking spaces for a local business. Pictured in front of the house from left to right are Jay Shultus, Anna Dedrick Lincoln, Levi Dedrick, Clara Burnham, Beulah Dedrick, and Eva Carlton Dedrick. (Courtesy of Thelma Scott.)

The home of Walter J. Pitkin was built about 1892. The wide-open porch was very fashionable. Pitkin family members pictured from left to right are Walter J., Myra, Alice, Allison, and Corliss. This house was later home to Charles Cudney, who had the livery stable here and an autobus line. This house stands on the corner of Center and Mechanic Streets.

This house still stands on Palmer Avenue. It was the home of John T. Rice and his wife, Agnes, and was built in the late 1800s. Rice was a supervisor of Corinth, school commissioner for the second district, and elder at the Presbyterian church. This house had a splendid fence surrounding it with a hitching post in front. The barn to the left was made into an apartment house.

Residence of Warren Curtis   Palmer and Corinth, N. Y.

The residence of Warren and Margaret Parmenter Curtis stood on Palmer Avenue in front of the current town hall. It was built about 1890 of the best material and plumbing. The grounds were artistically landscaped. The Curtis family had a winter residence on Main Street, and this one was their summer home. The home was given to the town by their daughters to become the Corinth Hospital, and it was razed in 1972.

Margaret Parmenter Curtis was born in Corinth in 1848. Her grandparents were early settlers of the community. She taught school until her marriage to Warren Curtis, and 5 of the 10 children born to the couple died in infancy. She was the organist at the Baptist church. She died in 1931.

For many years, this house on Palmer Avenue was the home of the paper mill manager. A tennis court was located to the right of the building. Eventually the house was sold to become a private residence and is now also used as a realty office and home.

The Bilodeau house stood on the corner of Pine and Sixth Streets and was built in the late 1800s by a Mr. White. This house burned in the 1970s. (Courtesy of the Saratoga County Historian's Office.)

The Riley S. Mallery home still stands on Main Street opposite the Methodist church. This brick house was built about 1900. In 1906, Mallery was a Democratic candidate for town supervisor. (Courtesy of the Saratoga County Historian's Office.)

Ella Eggleston Andrew and her husband, Peleg Andrew, are standing at the front of their home on Mallery Street about 1900. He operated a wagon shop next door to this home for over 45 years.

This brick house on Palmer Avenue was built in the 1890s during the housing boom in Corinth. (Courtesy of the Saratoga County Historian's Office.)

This farmhouse stands on South Main Street between Fuller and Hack Roads. For many years, it was known as the DeLoriea farm. It was built in the mid-1800s and was once owned by the Ambler family. (Courtesy of the Saratoga County Historian's Office.)

The Young's place stood on Clothier Road and was built in the mid-1800s. The sign over the porch advertises root beer for sale by Arthur G. Young. He made deliveries throughout town in the 1890s. The woman standing behind the baby is Cora Aldrich Young, and the baby is Maud Young.

The Ambrose Clothier place stands on Folts Road and was built about 1830 close to the Hudson River. Its owners included Marco Davis and Christine Robinson. (Courtesy of the Saratoga County Historian's Office.)

Residence of Mrs. J. A. Jacobie
Palmer, N. Y.

Mrs. J. A. Jacobie was the postmistress for Palmer for more than 25 years. Mead's store was located next door. The house stands on Palmer Avenue between Sixth and Heath Streets.

In 20 years, not much changed on Main Street. The image above shows the primary road through town about 1900. The picture below shows the street looking north about 1925 after it was paved.

Main Street, Corinth, N. Y.

Louis A. Parmenter is shown here with his goat cart at his home on Palmer Avenue about 1890. After attending Corinth schools, he went to Cornell University School of Medicine and returned to Corinth in 1906 to practice medicine. He was also the doctor for the International Paper Company for several decades, as well as the health officer for the town and physician for the Corinth Public School System. He died in 1967.

The railroad station for Corinth was located one mile out of town off Hamilton Avenue. This building was replaced by a newer depot in 1911.

Four

CORINTH
IN THE MILITARY

Corinth has always contributed to the military effort. Several of the early settlers were veterans of the American Revolution. Some fought at Saratoga and returned with their families to the area after the war ceased. One Hessian soldier, John Purqua, who fought on the British side and defected to the American side at Saratoga, came to settle along a Native American trail near South Corinth. Three men from Corinth were involved in the War of 1812. During times of peace, many men were members of the militia. The Civil War saw nearly 160 men join the military, and many died from disease, wounds, and imprisonment. Most returned home, some with wounds that never healed. The Spanish-American War had two soldiers from Corinth enlist. Over 100 men from Corinth answered the call to arms for World War I, and more than 600 men and women joined the armed forces during World War II. Only a few years later, 30 Corinthians were involved in the Korean conflict. Two were held as prisoners of war. Vietnam was another conflict that saw many Corinthians in the military service. More recently, Desert Storm and the Iraqi and Afghanistan wars have seen Corinth citizens head off to war. Corinth has always shown its patriotism both at home and on the front lines.

Adam Comstock was a colonel during the American Revolution and served with Gen. George Washington during Valley Forge. In 1996, through the efforts of World War II veteran Victor Orto, a commemorative plaque was erected near Comstock's homestead.

BURIAL SITE
OF

COL. ADAM COMSTOCK
REV. WAR SOLDIER
D.O.B. 1740 – 1819

APPOINTED BY
GOV. DEWITT CLINTON
AS CHARIMAN OF
COMMITTEE THAT
ESTABLISHED THE NEW
YORK STATE PUBLIC
SCHOOL SYSTEM.

John Purqua settled in the vicinity of South Corinth in 1793, coming from Rhode Island. Purqua was born in Germany and impressed into military service and made a mercenary to the British army. While fighting at Saratoga, he deserted by swimming across the Hudson River and joining Gen. Horatio Gates's army. This house at the corner of Wells Road and Route 9N was probably built by his son.

The recruiting station during the Civil War was located in this building, which later became Rich Allen's Auto Supply store. The recruiter set up a small table area in the corner of a shop and signed men up for service. (Courtesy of the Saratoga County Historian's Office.)

Pvt. Philip Rice of the 30th New York Infantry was the first to enlist in the Civil War from Corinth in 1861. During his service, he was promoted to second lieutenant. He fought at the Second Battle of Bull Run, where he was killed in action at Groveton. This gave him the unfortunate honor of being the first Corinthian killed in the Civil War.

James S. Clothier and his sister Sarah Jane posed for the photographer soon after his enlistment. He was a private in Company D, 77th New York Infantry. He died of typhoid fever on June 12, 1862.

Ambrose C. Hickok was a private in the 115th New York Infantry, having enlisted in 1862. He was later transferred to the invalid corps. Discharged with a rank of sergeant, he was part of the honor guard for Pres. Abraham Lincoln's funeral train. Upon returning to Corinth, he helped organize the Grand Army of the Republic, a group for Civil War veterans.

Veterans Of War Of '61-'65

Who Enlisted from the Town
of Corinth, Saratoga Co. N. Y.,

Darius Martin.
Luther Frazier.
Chauncy Gilbert Ide.
Clark Doty.
David Howe.
William Morgan Clothier.
Ransom Sacket Kingsley.
George Washington Howe.
James Sanford Clothier.
Dallas Fraker Paul.
Alonzo Allen.
Benjamin Wheaton.
Nathan Ide.
William Orson Jackson.
Alexander Walker.
Jesse Ferbush Wood.
Lorenzo Mallery.
Henry William Stearns.
Ransom Varney.
Edgar Varney.
James Brown Varney.
Isaac Plue.
Presby Corlew.
Edgar Gallup.
John St. John.
Sylvester Andrew.
John Merritt.
Sidney Thomson Viele.
William Woodard.
Hugh McConhie, Sr.
Joseph McConhie.
Hugh McConhie, Jr.
George McConhie.
Alexander Showers.
Joseph Showers.
Thomas Dwight Combs.
Justin Nelson Combs.
George James Place.
Charles Payne Chapman.
Elijah Earles, Jr.
Frederick Edward Parkman.
Ambrose Woodard.
William Pettit Lyon.

David Trap Burnham.
John Rhodes Place.
James Earley.
Harvey William Barrass.
Charles Wesley Davis.
George Lyon.
James Turner.
Roe Willard Mason.
Harmon Hagadorn.
George Hagadorn.
Daniel Webster Kendall.
Frederick William Andrews.
William Nevins Herrick.
George Washington Brooks.
Archibald Brooks.
Daniel Cady.
John Henry Demming.
John Redman.
Luman Gray.
Levi McIntosh.
Epaphroditus Walker.
Harillak Jerome Loop.
Reuben Varney.
Peter Denel.
Alonzo Dunn.
Thomas Herrick.
Myron Wade Wilcox.
Robert Herrick.
Hiram Woodcock.
James Henry Woodcock.
Levi Manning.
David Lewis Walker.
John Herrick.
Frances Romain Walker.
Benjamin Young.
Henry William Cass.
Solomon Heman Hickok.
Ambrose Clothier Hickok.
Theodorus Older.
Emmet Lake.
Henry Brower.
Philip Rice.
Uriah Young.

Horace Ballaw.
David Lewis Kinney.
Daniel Webster Raymond.
Andrew Jackson Keys.
George Wendell.
Augustur Sherman.
Chancy Searls.
Timothy Brower.
Daniel B. Ide.
Thomas McCarthy.
Emery White.
Richard Clothier.
Henry Davis.
John Smith.
James Graham.
Alexander Richardson.
Abraham Cunningham.
John Stewart.
Karl Peck.
David Fitzgerald.
Orison Gallop.
Jeremiah Sayres.
Alonzo Whittemore.
Dyer P. Riex.
Joseph Thyer.
Henry Beach.
Edward Ball.
Peter Conley.
Edward Wayman.
Francis Parrott.
John Noow.
Jacob Willer.
Nriah Hawkins.
Isaac E. Randall.
Orson Lindsey.
Francis Brower.
Darius Scofield.
Henry Mallery.
John Mack Master.
Aaron Brott.
John Brott.
Russel Varney.
Sidney Gray.

This list was posted in Corinth after the Civil War. One of the soldiers who was severely wounded during the war was Ransford Densmore. During the battle of Hanover Courthouse, he was shot in the head and remained unconscious for three weeks. The wound never fully healed, and his head had to be rebandaged each day until his death, over 50 years later.

Pvt. Henry Mallery enlisted in 1862 from Corinth and served in the 115th New York Infantry. He was taken prisoner with his regiment at Harper's Ferry and later paroled. He was discharged with his regiment in 1865.

The Grand Army of the Republic prepare for a parade on Main Street in the 1880s. The original clapboard Baptist church can be seen at the far right.

The Civil War monument was dedicated on July 4, 1908. Originally it stood in the center of the intersection of Main and Maple Streets. In the 1920s, it was moved to the beach. Now it stands in front of the Corinth Town Hall on Palmer Avenue. During the 1908 unveiling ceremony, U.S. Supreme Court justice James W. Houghton said that during the Civil War, "the Town was poor in everything but patriotism, having sent two out of every seven of its male population to the front."

Henry Tucker was a Corinth volunteer in the Spanish-American War in 1898. He served for about four months. In this 1970 photograph, 97-year-old Tucker is pictured with Rufus Randall (center) and Lester Tucker (right).

Charles Miles (left), George Melville, and John Rotherham (seated in front) are pictured in 1918. Rotherham was a sergeant major in the artillery in World War I. He later served as village trustee and then mayor from 1935 to 1939. Melville was mayor from 1924 until 1931.

A parade was held on July 4, 1919, to welcome the return of the soldiers from World War I. Frank St. John decorated his truck for the parade.

The lineup of soldiers and sailors was photographed on Main Street on July 4, 1919. Over 100 Corinthians served in World War I. Leon Siegel was the first casualty from the area, having died of pneumonia in France. Horace Washburn and Ray VanDenburg were the first two to be killed in battle. (Courtesy of J. Douglas Anderson.)

The World War I honor roll was erected on Main Street in the village of Corinth in 1918. Originally 37 Corinthians enlisted at the outset of World War I. Many residents went to other communities to sign up, and several veterans settled in Corinth after the war.

The Corinth roll of honor for World War II was erected at the foot of schoolhouse hill on Palmer Avenue. The names that were preceded with gold stars were those who died while serving their country. The sign was eventually dismantled and stored in the EMBA hall and later disposed of.

This banner hung in the window of the family of Arthur Allen of River Street during World War II. He was a flight officer in the air corps and was killed on March 16, 1945, when his plane went into the Mediterranean Sea.

During the Korean conflict, two Corinth soldiers were taken as prisoners of war and later released in the middle of 1953. A large parade and celebration was held for them on September 27, 1953. They are shown riding in the parade; M.Sgt. Edwin H. Potter is on the left, and M.Sgt. Gordon Petro is on the right.

The community celebrated the end of Operation Desert Storm on July 4, 1991, with a parade and celebration. One Corinth High School graduate who did not come home was Otto Clark. He was a member of Delta Force and was killed in a Black Hawk helicopter crash when returning from a scud-hunting mission in Iraq on February 21, 1991.

This honor roll was erected in front of the Corinth Town Hall for the men and women who are serving the country in Operation Enduring Freedom.

Five

ENTERTAINMENT AND RECREATION

The people of Corinth knew how to work hard and also enjoy a good time. In the early years, residents provided their own entertainment, and neighbors gathered for a picnic or music. Eventually performing groups came to town, and then entertainment businesses were established. On the weekends, hotels and clubs held special events, including music, drama, and dance. Lectures became a popular form of education and entertainment. The Corinth Free Library also served this dual purpose. Over the years, there have been dance halls, an opera house, bowling alleys, ball fields, sports, camps, fraternal organizations, flying clubs, scout groups, lectures, celebrations of all kinds, and the recreational opportunities offered by the Hudson River. The river is what brought people to Corinth in the first place and also provided them with endless hours of fun and relaxation. The river continues to be a central focus for recreation in the community. Corinthians knew how to amuse themselves and captured some of those moments on film for all to enjoy.

The German American Club stood near the end of Pine Street. It was an impressive three-story structure erected about 1880 by Luther Smith. A stock company of German Americans organized and wanted a club for the many Germans that had come to Corinth to work in the paper mill. The building contained an opera hall, bowling alley, pocket billiard parlor, reception room, basketball court, and boarding rooms. The Germans also had their own health benefit society for members. During World War I, the name was changed to the Club because of anti-German sentiment and was later managed by an Irish family named Flynn. On July 4, 1919, it burned to the ground and was believed to be the result of a defective light in the stock room. The loss of the building was estimated at $15,000.

The Central Opera House was located behind the Central House Hotel on Center Street. It was built by J. G. Lawler in 1896 and 1897, and was one story in height, measuring 100-by-50 feet. Alfred Mallery purchased the property in 1906 and started showing silent movies there soon after. The theater shown here on the left side of the street burned down in December 1916.

STARR THEATRE
CENTER STREET   CORINTH, N. Y.
R. C. A. SOUND SYSTEM
PROGRAM WEEK OCT. 19, 1936

MON-TUES., OCT. 19-20
DOUBLE FEATURE
PETER B. KYNE WESTERN STORY
"THE GALLANT DEFENDER"
PLUS
"THE JONES FAMILY EDUCATING FATHER"
Betty Boop Cartoon—"We Did It"
2 SHOWS 7.00-9.15

WED-THURS., OCT. 21-22
DOUBLE FEATURE
GEO. RAFT-DELORES COSTELLO IN
"YOURS FOR THE ASKING"
PLUS
WM. GARGAN-CLAIR DODD IN
"NAVY BORN"
Popeye Cartoon— "Lets Get Moving"
2 SHOWS 7.00-9.15

FRI-SAT. OCT. 23-24
WARNER BROS SPECIAL PRODUCTION
"ANTHONY ADVERSE"
STARRING FREDERIC MARCH-OLIVIA DE HAVILAND
Colored Merrie Melodies—"Let It Be Me"
2 SHOWS 7.00-9.15   15c MATINEE SATURDAY 2:30 P. M

COMING NEXT WEEK
MON-TUES.
"Country Beyond" and "Panic In The Air"
WED-THURS.
"Broadway Hostess" and "Return of Sophie Lang"
FRI-SAT
"Sing, Baby Sing" and New Serial "Flash Gordon"
with Buster Crabbe

The Starr Theatre was rebuilt on the site of the opera house by Mallery. It was named for Frances Starr, a well-known actress and niece of Mallery's wife. The first talking picture show was presented here in 1930. The theater was torn down to make way for a new banking complex in 1970. This program is from October 1936.

The old store in South Corinth stood across the road from Eno's store. It was called Densmore's Hall and was run by William Eggleston. Upstairs there was a large room where fraternal organizations held their meetings. A glass blower once demonstrated here.

A group of South Corinth bicyclists gather in front of Eggleston's store. Cycling was a popular hobby. In 1892, J. A. Dayton's store in Corinth advertised that it sold the best bicycles on the market. (Courtesy of Mary Earls.)

In the 1930s, the D'Avignon's Bowling Alley was operated on Main Street under what later became Waring's Pharmacy. The members of the local bowling league from left to right are Ken Smith, Bill Miller, Irwin White, Harold "Bus" Waldron, Jimmy Doherty, Harold Clayton, and Howard Forbirger.

The International Paper Company ball team sits for a picture in 1920. Many Corinth residents turned out to see their favorite team play against visitors. The team members from left to right are (first row) "Lanky" Plue, Emerson Barber, "Stub" Meader, "Buck" Cohan, Harold Connolly, and Johnny Crumpler; (second row) Frank Ingraham, Dick Ormsby, Charlie Diedrich, "Cappy" Ross, Jack Cohan, Johnny Cohan, and "Dolly" Lyons.

This photograph of the semiprofessional baseball team was taken in 1947. Team members from left to right are (first row) John Atwell, Sam Bronzene, Harry Burdick, Don Stanton, and James Doherty; (second row) Bill Doherty, unidentified, Ken Fitzgerald, George Doherty, Barney Donovan, Bob Collins, and Wilson Smead; (third row) Bus Waldron, Alvin Barney, Duff Doherty, Gerald Frasier, Don Boutelle, Banjo Frasier, Huck Rollman, and Bill Banks.

Seen here from left to right, Mrs. Paul Yanik, Ed Green, and Paul Yanik caught their limit of pike at Stewart's Dam in the fall of 1955. Their proud picture appeared in the local EMBA paper.

114

Camp Mesacosa was located at Efnor Lake in the northwest corner of Corinth. Dr. Jesse Williams, a professor at Teacher's College at Columbia University, first operated the camp. Later it was run as a girls' camp by Miss Sanford. Swimming instruction, boating, and nature crafts were part of the curriculum, as well as dancing, music, and dramatics. Elaborate plays were presented to the community each year by the campers. The property consisted of over 400 acres and more than two miles of lake frontage. The camp was in operation for more than 50 years and closed in the mid-1970s.

Camp Gahada at Lake Tawiskarou in the Adirondacks was a boys' camp started by William B. Efner Sr., Gus Huthsteiner, and Chatfield Bates in 1909 at Jenny Lake. Many of the boys came from Schenectady to enjoy trout fishing, rock climbing, tennis, swimming, and boating. The dining hall shows the boys ready for mealtime. The two woodstoves were used to cook and bake meals during the hottest months of the summer. Ida Hamm did the cooking and cleaning with help from her daughters Frances and Lida. Hamm's husband, William, was the caretaker of the camp. It closed in 1917 at the beginning of World War I.

Corinth had several Irish immigrant families. Many of them settled along lower Palmer Avenue and onto Eastern Avenue. This area was referred to as "Cork Town" because so many of the families had emigrated from County Cork in Ireland. A chapter of the Ancient Order of Hibernians was founded in Palmer in the late 1800s. Posing in Saratoga Springs in 1896, the organization included the Mildes Band as well other members of the group.

The Daughters of America, McGregor Council, was organized in 1912. The patriotic organization helped support a home for the aged, an orphans' fund, and provided death benefits for its members. This photograph taken in 1916 in the Odd Fellows hall on Maple Street included the first council officers. The man in the middle is William Quinn, a trustee.

Shorey's Military Band was a popular music group in the early 1900s. The band members are, from left to right, (first row) ? Cooney, ? Heinz, ? Butler, ? Connors, E. Brown, L. Eddy, and Harry Shorey; (second row) ? Lake, C. Richardson, W. Kendall, ? Connors, A. Woodruff, and C. Simmons; (third row) Howard Pitkin, G. Roberts, H. Young, L. Hughes, J. Montgomery, and B. Robinson.

118

Clarence Flora was the first Corinthian to own an airplane. His Waco biplane was purchased in 1928. He flew an airmail flight to Albany as a promotional event for the postal service in 1938. Ralph "Pop" Pease (left), Waco the dog, and Flora are pictured here in front of the plane. (Courtesy of Ernest Clothier.)

The Twin Falls Flying Club was located at the airstrip at the end of Eggleston Street on the property of Joe Seppa. It was in operation from the 1940s through the 1960s. The area is developed now and has many houses on it.

An early Boy Scout troop is pictured on the steps of the Corinth Village Hall in the 1920s, within a few years of its founding in Corinth. The leader was Victor Parmenter, seen in the center of the third row. Glenn Barber is third from the left in the first row, and Phil Newton is on the right side of the third row.

The Corinth Girl Scouts were photographed on Hamilton Avenue in the 1920s. Their meetings were held in the Pitkin building, and dues were 5¢ a meeting. The Corinth troop was organized on September 27, 1918. They bought and helped sell liberty bonds and held food sales, dances, and parties.

The Maschmedt family moved to Corinth in 1893 and purchased the Thomas Carpenter farm on Heath Road. They established a Theosophist society at their farm, which combined science, philosophy, and religion. Lectures were held at the farm that drew 300 people. A vegetarian diet was stressed because meat eating was considered evil. The local clergy spoke out against the group each week in the paper. Mr. Maschmedt bought a store in town and planned to open a perfumery factory. By 1896, the family sold out and started conducting lectures at Saratoga Springs.

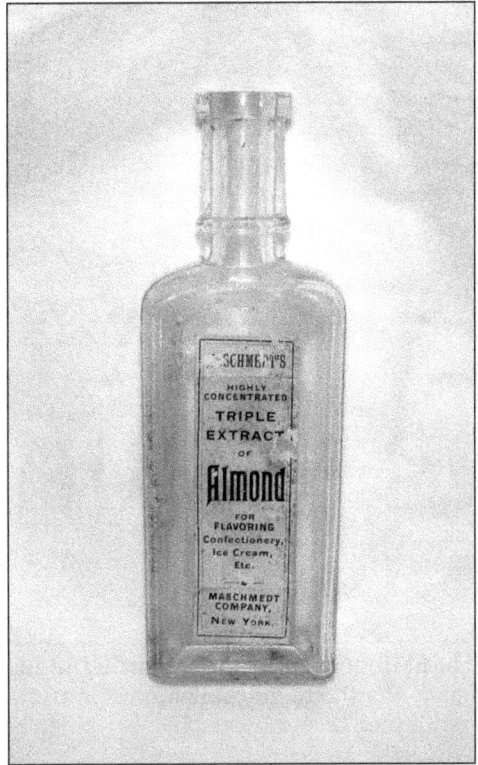

The Boggs farm was home to the Corinth Bluegrass Festival in the 1970s and 1980s. Several well-known performers sang here. Donald Boggs and his wife, Winnie, moved here with their family from the Catskills in 1946. Jim Gill operated a dairy farm here in the 1930s and built tourist cabins along Route 9N. Currently the home is owned by the Edward Byrnes family.

The EMBA presented boxing matches for area youth at its hall. Seated second from left is trainer Jimmy Monthony. Joe Hanlon, chief instructor and referee, is shown with his back to the camera in this June 1956 photograph.

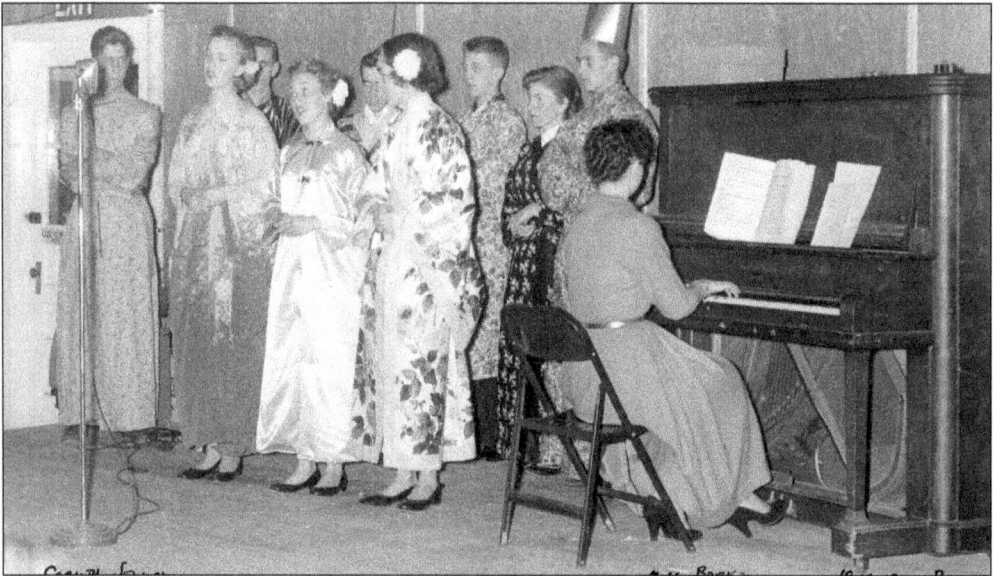

The Corinth High School seniors sang excerpts from the play *The Mikado* in 1955. They provided entertainment for the third-annual retired and 25 year employees party. The operetta had previously been performed at the school. Lois Barker accompanied the group.

The ice-skaters had a wonderful time on the rink near the Curtis Mill in December 1955. George Duell had worked hard to get the rink ready. Judy Baugh is the center skater.

The Corinth Wheelers were dedicated to deter reckless driving in town. Founded in 1956, they wanted to help reduce highway accidents. The members pictured in the fall of 1957 from left to right are William Cowles, Jerry Matoon, Warren Post, Ken Guilder, Carol Guilder, Jean Brannon, Bob Kelly, Emerson Cowles Jr., Curtis Mills, and Raymond Fuller. Other members not in the picture were Leonard Anderson and Corky Shattuck.

Entertainment for the 50th anniversary picnic of the International Paper Company in June 1948 was provided by local artists, including the Sitts Sisters and the Three S's. Pictured here are Thomas Wheaton, George Melville, George Faller, Joseph Forte, Gerald Galasham, Mr. Mosher, George Mallery, Tommy Sullivan, Tommy Smith, Jimmie Smith, and Judy Holland.

The minstrel show presented by the Catholic Daughters of America in 1969 starred, from left to right, (seated) Frances Cromie and George Plant; (standing) Thomas Cromie, Ralph Bordeau, Elizabeth Wilkins, George Doody, Gene Hanlon, and Fonzi Yannaci. All of the men except Yannaci were retired Hudson River International Paper Mill employees.

A huge celebration cake was created by home economics teachers from throughout Saratoga County for the June 14, 1976, parade and festivities during the bicentennial celebration. Each township was represented by a separate cake. Joan Welch, Corinth Central School home economics teacher and chairwoman of the Corinth Historical Commission, coordinated the event. She is shown standing here with David Meager of the Saratoga County Board of Supervisors and Corinth town supervisor Harry Waring (right).

Pagenstecher Park was presented to the village in 1919 by the heirs of Albrecht Pagenstecher, who had been president of the Hudson River Pulp and Paper Company. The park, which overlooks the Hudson River and Palisades, once had tame dear penned there during the summer months. After years of neglect, the park was cleaned up and rededicated in 1988.

The Corinth Free Library was first established in 1926. It opened in 1927 in a building located next to the shirt factory. Mabel Pitkin served as librarian for over 35 years. After another move, the library opened in its current building on Main Street in 1951. It is a living memorial to honor all who served in the world wars.

The beach and dock on the Hudson River has been a popular swimming area for generations. More than 200 years ago, this portion of the Hudson River was used by the Jessup brothers to land their logs before they went over the falls, and it became known as Jessup's Landing. Mount Anthony can be seen in the distance.

Albert Clothier is pictured heading upstream at Clothier Hollow about 1960. He built and rented rowboats of his own design for $1 a day. (Courtesy of Ernest Clothier.)

Visit us at
arcadiapublishing.com

www.ingramcontent.com/pod-product-compliance
Lightning Source LLC
Chambersburg PA
CBHW080615110426

42813CB00006B/1519